Mulga parrot

Blue-billed duck

Swamp wallaby

Great desert skink

Common wallaroo

Freshwater crocodile

Red-necked pademelon

Dingo

Long-nosed potoroo

Numbat

Marsupial mole

Crest-tailed mulgara

Perentie

Northern nailtail wallaby

Children's python

Central bearded dragon

Whiptail wallaby

Spinifex pigeon

Common wombat

Emu

T0018360

For every copy of this book sold, a donation will
be made to WIRES, the New South Wales Wildlife
Information, Rescue and Education Service.

One Day on Our Blue Planet … In the Outback © Flying Eye Books 2020.

First edition published in 2020 by Flying Eye Books, an imprint
of Nobrow Ltd. 27 Westgate Street, London, E8 3RL.

Text and illustrations © Ella Bailey 2020.
Ella Bailey has asserted her right under the Copyright, Designs and
Patents Act, 1988, to be identified as the Author and Illustrator of this Work.

1 3 5 7 9 10 8 6 4 2

Published in the US by Nobrow (US) Inc.
Printed in Poland on FSC® certified paper.

MIX
Paper from
responsible sources
FSC® C001693

ISBN: 978-1-912497-20-1

www.flyingeyebooks.com

Ella Bailey

ONE DAY
ON OUR
BLUE PLANET

...IN THE OUTBACK

Flying Eye Books
London | New York

As the fiery sun rises over the dry grasslands of the wild Australian outback, a little red kangaroo peers out from his mother's pouch.

The members of his small mob are lounging and playing around him.

Here's his mother and the other does ...

... and there are the other joeys.

Over here, the towering buck with bright red fur is his father.

Like all marsupials, his mother has carried him around in the pouch on her stomach since he was just the size of a small bean.

Kangaroos eat grass and shrubs, but there has been no rain here and food is growing scarce. The kangaroos must set out in search of fresh grasslands to graze on.

The joey's mother tightens her stomach muscles to keep her baby secure as they journey past looming red rocks ...

... and through vast dusty deserts.

Adult kangaroos use their strong, muscular legs to cover large distances in very few leaps.

When the midday sun gets too hot, the kangaroos shelter in the shade of a lonely tree, licking their forearms to stay cool.

But this curious joey is bored of sitting around.
He decides to venture out of his mother's pouch to explore.

Over there, a short-beaked
echidna munches on ants ...

... and here, a blue-tongued
lizard basks in the heat.

And over here ... WATCH OUT!

The joey dives back into his mother's pouch.

This lone dingo is no match for an adult kangaroo's powerful kick!

The mob moves on, eager to find some green grass soon.
They pass some eucalyptus trees, where koalas are munching on the tasty leaves.

Finally, they make it!

Water is scarce in the outback so countless creatures have
gathered by this billabong. Kangaroos don't need to drink often,
but this is much needed after their day of travelling in the bright sun.

As the last heat of the day fades away, many new nocturnal critters emerge. The kangaroos will also graze throughout the cooler night.

But this little joey is tired after his busy day.
He settles down to drink his mother's milk
in the comfort of her pouch ...

... until the red sun rises again, on another day on our blue planet.

ANIMALS OF THE AUSTRALIAN OUTBACK
UP HIGH

Brolga

Red-tailed
black-cockatoo

Green tree
snake

Laughing
kookaburra

Koala

Mistletoebird

Crested bellbird

Southern boobook

Splendid
fairy-wren

Budgerigar

Little corella

Wedge-tailed eagle

Australian
white ibis

Black swan